MORNING IN SERRA MATTU

MORNING IN SERRA MATTU

A NUBIAN ODE

as told to E.G. Dubovsky who recorded it in verse

ARIF GAMAL

McSWEENEY'S
POETRY SERIES

For
Zeine, Fanna, Jamal, Rami

and the children of all
dam-affected people

M^CSWEENEY'S

SAN FRANCISCO

www.mcsweeneys.net

Copyright © 2014 Arif Gamal

Cover art and frontispiece by Dadu Shin.

The McSweeney's Poetry Series is edited by Dominic Luxford and Jesse Nathan.

The editors wish to thank assistant editor Rachel Z. Arndt, editorial interns
Alison Castleman, Andrew Colarusso, Caroline Crew, Jess Bergman, Neesa Sonoquie,
and copyeditor Britta Ameel.

ISBN 978-1-938073-89-2

Printed by Thomson-Shore in Michigan.

A precedent for *Morning in Serra Mattu* may be found in the Indian epic poem *The Mahābhārata*. Vyasa narrates that story to the scribe Ganesha, who writes everything down, including his own questions and some commentary, while addressing the narrator as 'you.' —A.G.

Father of author, Jamal Mohammed Ahmed,
Sudanese amabasador to the UK. London, 1964.

Nura, author's aunt-in-law, and her daughter, Fatima.
Suarda-Mahas, 1948.

Author (seated far right) with brothers, sisters, and cousin. Khartoum, 1953.

Author's brothers, Jamal (seated) and Mahjoub. Cairo, c. 1934.

Black Madonna excavated at Faras, near Serra Mattu.

Gamal M. Ahmed
P. O. Box 1605 Khartoum
Tel. 43628

جمال محمد احمد
ص. ب. ١٦٠٥/الخرطوم
تلفون ٤٣٦٢٨

٤/٢٦

بدون مقدمة، ما استطعت الكتابة اليك، لأن قلبي مضطرب
في غير ما شيء. انتهى نصف ثقة الايمان برب بعض الاحايين. لا أعرف
مصدراً للقلق. فان بجانبي زمانا واحد من أحب الناس. أكاد
لا أحصي مصادر السعد عندي، وأعرف مئات من الناس تغبطني
عليه، لأني أعرف سبب هذا القلق. أرده لضعف الايمان عندي.
ضعف الايمان سببه أني أومن بالذي علمتني إياه تجاربي وقراءاتي،
وما ذاك ايمان يعين على هدوء البال. غير إيمان هو ذاك
الذي يحمله طموحاً، ولا تحسبه اني أقصد "ايمان العجائز"
الذي يقول به البلهاء، إيمان تماماً وفاتتك زهرة، أنا أقصد
الايمان الذي تقبله بعد بحث في دخيلة نفسك وتأمل في الذي
يقع حواليك ولك. ينجح الذين حواليك ويخفقون، وتنجح أنت
وتخفق في خطواتي للتقدم وخطواتك للامام. تتدبر كل هذا
ساعات تخلو لنفسك بعيداً من "الزحام المجنون". إن كنت
من أشباه توماس هاردي الذي عاش التجربة وكتب رواية
"بعيداً من الزحام المجنون" وستجد أشباهه في محيط اختصاصك.
ما أنجب كثيراً الذين تركوا الحوادث تجرفهم هنا وهناك لا
يملكون من أمرهم شيئاً، إنهم في شغل عن أنفسهم بالذي يجدونه
حولهم، لا يعون يجدون الذي يريدون.

٤/٢٧

كان الذي قرأته الآن ضحى أمس وما تيسر لي أن أتم لأن حسين
شريف وعلي عبد القيوم دخلا علي من ... وجلست اليهم، فضاع
خط تفكيري الليلة، وأحب ان أقف عند بعض النقاط العملية قبل
أن يجيء محمد سيد أو صديق ابراهيم عوض:

- اتتك ٤ ظروف من الجامعة فيها مثل هذا النموذج الذي
ارسله لك كي تطلب اليهم أن يرسلوا لك منشوراتهم حيث
انت، إن كانت منشورات تحب أن تطلع عليها
- اتت رسالة مسجلة من سوريا وتعذر استلامها حتى
حين - حتى انا استلمها نيابة عنك. اتحاد البريد السوداني

Letter from author's father to author. April 26, 1980.

CONTENTS

I.
TALL PALMS

TALL PALMS

they grew high
their roots stood above the ground
in gnarled entwine

and under one quite lofty tree
beneath the lifted snarl
the long one lived
thick languid quiet
with a flickery tongue

the boy never saw the whole length of him

the house was huge
like a palace fifty yards in width alone
with high mud walls and an inner courtyard
where the tall palms stood

and every day after the goats were milked
before anything else was done
Fatima took a large full bowl
and set it down beneath the palm

and slowly lifting his patterned body
the boa came up from the earth
beneath the column
and wound himself around the writhing root

tongue flickering from the tapering head
he lowered to the silky drink

the bowl was empty in a flash
and the snake turned quickly to shadow
though each time stopping once and looking back
at Fatima before he vanished

she was your grandmother
and written of in the book
of the Sudan
as an example of strong women
who guided men in that country
especially among the Nubian

and she was the mother
the book went on
of Jamal Mohamed Ahmed
well known by all by then
and he was your father

and when he was a boy he never felt such fear
and such thrill as when he followed his mother
close behind her steps
as she carried the large bowl
of milk
across the yard

to feed the snake

and never did he see
he said
the whole length of it

NO ENMITY

Fatima was up by dawn
before in fact the dark was gone
sweeping gently the walls and floor

not to injure with a broom
but to encourage the scorpions
to leave the house where they spent the night
and to go out again into the yard

in that whole family
in those generations
no one was ever injured by a scorpion
or by a snake
there was no enmity

and as for the snake
in those days
they did not wound its head
nor did it strike their heel

WASH EACH OTHER'S FACES

the Nile was the center of that Nubian village
Serra Mattu

and the houses all palatial dwellings
stood side by side in one long line
that paralleled the often gently wooded shore

facing west across fine white-grained sand
towards glimmering water that was like a sea

the betrothed couple would go down
and in ceremony wash each other's faces
and each other's hands
in the Nile

that was to them a blessing
with its gifts and treasures

THE NILE IS SILK

the banks are lush
with flourishing bush and wild acacia
and many tall date palms

the barefoot women walk in long jarjar
down a sandy path
to stand beside the river's edge

one woman eats a little rice
then hurls the rest into the Nile

one woman dips a golden ring for offering
to please the Nile god who gives fertility
though he is not the god of all

that's Nor
great Nor of old Nubia
and Kush and Meroë
all one
from long before the rule of pharaohs

Nor was loved and honoured along Nile sands
Nor was the one

what of Mohammed then and Allah
the Koran
one learns that now
but Nor is old

Islam is like a glaze on Nubia
where ways of Nor are old and deep
from long before the time of pharaohs

did Fatmareya pray as Muslims prayed?
she did
and made obeisance five times a day

but spoke of Nor
Nor's was the way
Nor reigned

A WEDDING

Fatima's husband had a former wife
a girl of trembling beauty
so admired and envied
that one spoke of the evil eye
that followed her

her first child even
was a boy

that stirred a new resentment
jealousy was the hidden word
no one knew the turmoil
in her hated soul

one night she rose
leaving her child on the bed
and fled to the river

she was found washed up on shore
and no one knew what or how
and then the child too died soon

'I have a daughter'
said a man from another town
'and she is shrewd and good'
they married her to the widower

you told how Fatima stood quietly
the whole ceremony

and you showed how she glanced intensely
here and there
head lowered

but without a word
holding in her vehement spirit
although it was hard yet to comprehend
what those faces meant
that you portrayed

FATIMA

this was Fatima
who came from another place
with her surging voice

she was never still
but telling people what to do and how
and she was always everywhere

if a fight occurred
she would be found in the middle of the stew
to give opinion and strong view

or she was home stirring up new orders
or doing business
she too knew how to sell goods and earn
and with the money she bought gold
she wore it on her arm
her voice churning in the household
and the village was never still

until one day the parents of her husband
came to him and said 'we will speak'

they sat underneath acacia trees
on straw mats near the river
the three together and the father
took out a knife before his son and said
'you must send this woman away
we do not want her

and if you do not do it
I will take this knife and stab my chest'

and his mother spoke
she lifted her breast and put it outside the robe
and with knife held up she told
if her son did not send away that wife
she would cut her breast

the son listened to his parents' words

the Nile moved by them
deep with current

and then he too took out a knife
and said he loved his wife
and would not send her off
and if his parents did those things he too
would cut away his life
and he returned to his house
where Fatima stood

she knew already what was said
and she raged at him

how could he speak thus
to his mother and his father
he should have obeyed and sent her off

some people tried to tell
she picked him up and took him in the room
and beat him for the insult to his parents

they came to love her too
and later when they were old
she cared for them with a strong tender nurture

. . .

a boy was born
Jamal
he grew and ran barefoot
along the sand and swam
the sky was vast

he knew to kneel in prayer
and followed his mother when she milked the goats
and when she brought the large full bowl
to set before the gnarled palm roots
where the great boa rose to drink

no one in those days in that family
was injured by a scorpion or snake
nor did they have many insects there
or any mice or rats

JAMAL

Jamal went to the little village school
and in the afternoon
he took his turn at the waterwheel
first harnessing the bull
then sitting in the seat and going round and round
right by the river

he was ten
his father and some other men had traveled north
to Egypt to work as janitors or cooks
to send money home to their families
while the women stayed at home
caring for the date palms
and making honey from the dates

you see it was a place
of milk and honey

in the old way
thus people lived

the Nubians were excellent cooks
and expert janitors
and Nubians were known especially
for honesty and truth

and while Jamal was tending the bull
who turned the waterwheel
he would hear from time to time

if the news was coming
thus they spoke of it
the news

the village was arranged in one long line
each house facing the Nile
across the sand

the news began in a soft wail
at one end or the other
and if it started in the north
a family that had someone working there in Egypt
rushed into their house and shut the door
and prayed that the noise getting louder and louder now
would stop before it reached them
or would pass them by

or if a family had someone working farther south
in a city in Sudan and the news
was coming from the path
it was they who ran into their houses
and shut their door

one day Jamal was seated at the turning wheel
the news coming from the north

he left the bull
and on his thin tan legs
he raced along the sand
to hide at home

THE WIDOW

one hundred and twenty-eight days
was the rule for a widow to sit
in the special shed of reeds
where other women could visit her
and sit and talk

thus Fatima 'sat'
with other women ringed about her
visiting

and one day her brother-in-law Suleiman
a man of often ill intent and twisted form
made his way to the wall of reeds
behind her seat

although he may not go within
he knew exactly where she was
and placed himself behind her
calling her name in a loud voice
and proclaiming that when the days to sit were over
she must think of no one else but marry him
it must be done

a widow was never permitted
and never did leave the widow's shelter
before her four months were finished
but Fatima rose up
and took a stick

the women rushed to hold her back
she shook them off with furious twists
and raced out the door to the place
where the arrogant man was seated
and she struck him with the stick
and lifted sand to fling upon him
more painful
with humiliation
than the blows

and she cried out in her strong voice
that from that time on her son Jamal
would be her husband and her son
and never never would she marry
any other man
nor may one even ask

JAMAL'S STUDIES

the hundred twenty-eight days finished
and Fatima returned home

then wise people spoke with her
saying she must marry once again
or how would she take care of her family

and she with indignant fervor
looked beyond their faces and above their heads
with a determination
she said she would take care
well enough

she traveled to her cousins
and gave the gold she wore to them
to hold in exchange for some money

then she bought a field
she knew when to plant and what was good

Jamal was finishing the village school
where he was best
and he had learned enough he said
to do what work there was in the village

his mother told him no he was not finished
he would go on to the other school
in town five miles from home

she bought him a gentle donkey
and he rode each day to school and back

he was again top student
and finally eighth grade was done
he graduated and came home to tell his mother
he was ready now to stay with her and work
to help her care for the whole family

she smacked him hard
'I don't want any favors' she said
'and when I need I'll ask'

she sent him off to the next school
where he was top as usual
and after several years he graduated
and told his mother
'now I am ready to stay with you and help'

'and what will you do here?' she asked him
'have the most important work' he said
'and what is that?' she asked

they both knew who was most important there
among the men who worked
the postman who would bring the letters
and who would write them to a far-off relative
'Abdul is ill now so come home'
'we need your help send money soon'

no said Fatima
a postman is not good enough

you must be
president

and off he went to school again
to Oxford on an isle
Britain

meanwhile the uncle Suleiman
who was a greedy and quite unpleasant man
was always troubling her
and even taking her to court
where women never went
to have the old parents live with him
although by then they preferred Fatima

and when the mayor showed equal equability
to both the litigants
'your words are sweet' and
'your words are like honey'
he said to each
fearing an enemy so near

Fatima rose in rage against the mayor
and lifting sand in her strong hands
she flung it in the mayor's face
and then went on to a higher court
and won the case and kept the parents
in her care with grace

TWO BEAUTIFUL GIRLS

one day Fatima saw
two lovely girls walking by
and claimed them right away

'no no' the people said
one is already engaged

she took her stick and ready to strike
went among the village folk
to announce peremptorily
that now the girls were hers
and if any dared make a claim
they'd feel her blows
no one opposed

she wrote her son to come home right away
and he obeyed
without knowing what or why

he learned on his arrival
that now was his engagement day
and when he saw the beauty of the fiancée
he did not argue

he and his brother were married
to the gracious girls their mother chose
and they lived happily

PART OF FAMILY

meanwhile Suleiman
the greedy uncle grown quite old
was still harassing Fatima
with much demand to give him this and that

and although married to a new young wife
he was much alone
no one would go near him
except Fatima who helped him live

and he sent endless messages of all the little things
and also big things that he needed
and she took care of him
because he was part of the family

thus they proceeded

II.

M BARAK

MBARAK

the struggle against Britain
took a toll on all
but was not bloody on the whole

although Jamal became covered by a lot of mud
hiding in the trenches
that the British dug as sewers
throughout Khartoum
to drain canals run from the Nile

and all of Africa was then enthralled
by Gandhi
holding him as a model even during the war

Jamal wrote long ferocious articles
attacking British rule
and signed 'Arif Said'
meaning 'I know happiness'

he demonstrated with 'ashika'
sitting in the street before the capital
and when police came
he had to hide in ditches

and once in nineteen forty-nine
emerging from the muddy trench
all covered with slime
and going home to wash

he found his family joyful at the door
congratulating him

'Mbarak Mbarak' they cried
'be blessed be blessed'

and he learned someone else had also just emerged
out of a slippery place

'you have a son' they rejoiced

'let him be called Arif'
said your father

KHARTOUM

soft grass is speaking to your feet

the first thing you remember in Khartoum
is not the huge old colonial house
the government appointed for your father
and his family when he was chosen
as the university's academic advisor

but the vast lawns where you ran barefoot
along banks of the diverted Nile branch
that wove among the tamarinds
and guavas grapefruit lemons
leaving silt

one lemon pressed
could fill a bowl with juice
and every kind of fruit grew lavishly
and shade trees
where you climbed in a rapture to the top

'Jenghis come here'
called your father's friend
he loved your wild abandonment
and called you Jenghis Khan

the grass spoke softly to your feet
with cool freshets of sweetness
unforgotten after many cities of both hemispheres

all their floors their plazas
and paved walkways canals streets

the backyard grasses of a far-off childhood
are still singing to your bare-soled feet

'Jenghis come in'
your father's friend called out
and you would rush to see them
they were geniuses
those friends that gathered round your father
for tumultuous speech of politics and literature

your love for him so great
that sometimes you were like a parent to a child
though he was grown and you were young
your love for him outdistanced time

you ran in and there he was
your father

THE BROTHERS

he read from when he woke up
very early in the morning
through several cups of tea before he rose

and always he had those funny little glasses on his nose
more toward the end of it than on the bridge
one saw him thus
it seemed he was almost always reading books
the house was filled with them
and later on he went back to his favorites
Dostoevsky Shakespeare Tolstoy

and you asked him why he read again
what he had already read
and he told how all of it was new
as he got older
and was changing as he changed

and then he'd tell you stories from the books
and stories from his life
such as about Ahmed your great-grandfather
and this is how it went

your great-grandfather had three sons
Mohammed
Hassan
and Suleiman

to Suleiman he said be like your brothers
and be good do well
but Suleiman would not listen
and went traveling to the hinterland on camelback
to sell little pieces of papers
with some words as amulets
he scribbled for their healing

though who knows what alchemy of faith
converted brass of commerce
into gold of health

and he had already been through two wives
with much unkindness
when one day he fell from his high camel
to the earth
incurring crippling injury
that left him twisted
as we saw him when paying court to Fatima

and Hassan
what of him?

Hassan was handsome as the stars
and when he walked he launched himself
with gallant stride and mighty chest
his shoulders rolling limberly

and his arms
in readiness for an embrace or war
swung rhythmically by his sides

his brow a prow of pride
cut through the waters of the air
and on his body
he wore clothing made of silk

to him his father said Hassan
the way you walk
it is not seemly
you must have more moderation and humility
and this silk all over you
it is not good
you need more humble plain material
of simple stuff

and Hassan said he would put away
the silken cloth
and wear plain weave
but as for how he walked
he told his father that God made him thus
he could not change

and to Mohammed your grandfather
then a young man
his father spoke and told him
that he did not know how it would be
or in what way
but he could only say
the children of Mohammed would be great

MAHJOUB

Mahjoub Mahjoub
where are you now
it's time for school

Mahjoub come right away
cried Fatmareya
which is Fatima daughter of Reya
her mother's name

come right away she cried

while running around the house and courtyard
searching for that second child
who troubled her so endlessly

and suddenly when glancing up
she spied him on the courtyard wall
thirty feet above the ground

oh the trouble that she had
with that rebellious willful boy

Mahjoub come down it's time for school

I'm not going

Yes you are

I'm not

You are

I'm not

oh why can't you be like your brother

I don't want to be like him
Jamal can go to school
I want to go to Cairo and live with Grandpa

oh the child was filled with useless dreams
you can't imagine what he wanted

tar and *asphalt*
he had heard the way the roads were covered
with such substances of odd sounding
never-before-heard names
which carried off his whole imagination

and unusual food he had not tasted
could be found
and something called the *movie*
where you went into an unconnected world
and there were ways there
one could make some money
for which he found he had a knack

she let him go

Cairo was vast complex thronging
and dense with endless wonder

Mahjoub started washing cars
and soon he found there was a Pasha
so began washing his

it was the time of Turkish rule
of the whole Middle East and Egypt
and the Pasha was immensely rich
and lived in endless excess

the example that you gave was how each day
he drank a little cup of soup
made from the juice of six or seven pigeons

and every day Mahjoub would come to wash the car
and the Pasha was immensely rich
but not too rich
to notice that bright Nubian boy
who came to wash the car
and he would pat his head and say kindly words
and give him a tariffe coin

Mahjoub enjoyed his city life
and after a while went home to Nubia
where he continued to be enterprising

from machines that he oiled
he built an empire of good repute
and from earth-moving equipment
he went to own properties

he had a touch
that brought envious success
and he became one of the richest men
in the Sudan

Magdi was the sacrificial lamb

II

one day in later life
Mahjoub was ill with dangerous plight
and traveled back to Cairo to the hospital
and resting in the hospital room
a doctor came
and told him there was another patient
who had no money
although he once was quite rich
in fact a Pasha
and everyone tried to treat him with the respect
to which he had been accustomed

though he couldn't pay for anything
and would Mahjoub agree to fund a room for him

what is the Pasha's name he asked
he said the name
it was the same

so bring him here Mahjoub instructed
and then the two were patients side by side
and talked at times
and Mahjoub asked do you remember

once a Nubian boy who washed your car each day
and you gave him a tariffe

oh let me think
I think I do
so long ago there was a Nubian boy
nice looking and good spirited
Mahjoub he was

yes it is I Mahjoub replied

and said then if the Pasha needed anything at all
he should ask him
Mahjoub would look after the things he needed
he was glad to do it

and later on Magdi told of all the things
Mahjoub had given away
and Magdi was the son of Mahjoub
everyone looked to for guidance
in a sensible way

he was not the eldest son
and he was happy off in London
studying computers
but when the family called
he came in his quiet mild way
and took the whole responsibility
they piled on his shoulders willingly
he was the one

and he told how it was after his father died
that every day the people came to him
and asked what happened
we did not receive the blankets
or the food or medicines
all kinds of things

and then the family learned
how every fall
Mahjoub sent truckloads of blankets and food to the north
where displaced Nubians
lived in the harsh desert climates
to which they were unaccustomed

or to the other lands
where displaced Nubians were sent after the colossal dam
reclaimed their lands

so many came he wondered if it was all true
but then he met the families
and learned how it was really so

and Magdi went on to give the things
his father Mahjoub had given
though in silence
so most never knew

MANGOS

you would run behind your father's house
across the lawns
beyond the shaved grass tennis courts
down to the cool diverted branch of Nile
with its dark chocolate silt
the gardeners dug to spread upon the beds
and there were lavish fruit trees
lush with leaves and fruit

but you would gaze through the dense
tamarind hedge full of forbidding thorn
to see how mangos then were getting on
in your British neighbor's
hundred-foot-high tree

gradually they changed from green
to yellow to a rosy ripening orange-red
you were approximately five
your brother Adil was twelve

together you ran down the length of tamarind wall
that ended at the Nile branch bank
where a six-foot fence of wood
was built over the hurrying silt-filled creek

your brother lifted you to the top
then went over himself
and helped you down

Adil climbed the tree
while you waited below with the skirts
of your light blue djellaba held forth
to catch the falling fruit
each large ripe orb releasing from the stem
as soon as touched

you would catch a few
then set them on the ground and catch some more
while contemplating the rich sweet tangy juices
soon to share

when something to the side began to feel a little odd
and looking up
all in a kind of khaki military garb
with shoulder flaps and many pockets
khaki shorts and high brown socks
brown shoes and pipe all thoroughly intimidating
and what's more with stick in hand

the British neighbor jumped from his back porch
and rushed you with a terrifying speed
though amused look

you fled with more than all your strength
and somehow though small
without your brother's help
negotiated the high six-foot fence to safety

Adil knew enough to remain still
in the dark high interior of the mango tree

unheard unseen
unthreatened for a period

you liked to think the neighbor would not strike you
though he ran at you and held the stick
and near the hedge of tamarind
was also the garage where sometimes you would play
because it was so cool inside

and it was only several days after the mango episode
you were wearing the light blue djellaba once again
and playing in the cool garage with sister and with brother
when behind the bent back door

you suddenly spied a heap of toys
small metal cars and trucks
and things you had never seen
you had no toys except the kind you made

you piled them in the outstretched skirt of your djellaba
and ran fast to the house wildly excited
with the others running close behind

and then later thought it must have been
the neighbor after all
who left the marvelous presents

you still have to ponder now it must have been
the neighbor

with the frightening stick

WITH ALAWIYYA

Alawiyya was your sister
one year older
with whom you loved to set out to explore
and together you knew all the roads
and hidden paths and complex secret passageways
of all those neighborhoods

sometimes climbing on roofs of garages
from which height you reached out with a wire
you bent with hook to pull
tamarinds down toward you
taking in your hands the fruit

and the British were quite crazy with such sun
to grow every kind of citrus that they could

to water with each moon
they flooded the gardens from the Nile
the orchard then became a lake

white and gray herons flew down to the trees
all kinds of birds
and some you never seem to see these days
and they would feed on frogs
and many kinds of insects
while you and Alawyya
wandered through the mirroring water
and gazed around and played among the birds
then whitening the orchard trees

while you waded deep in cool mud
and looking up beheld the long-legged
portents of longevity

they lofted in on open wings
white wide and light
to settle on the orchard trees and glide down
to the lake

that life is finding path akin to path

and bending in an elegant script
long winding throats and spears of beak
select frog or little fish
then lofting up
floating effortlessly on windless air
of African heat

they rose and soon enough were off again
to Nile banks whence they had come

or farther even
to deep interiors
maybe Burundi

'IT'S A DRESS'

'it's a dress a dress'
they jeered at Brummana school in Lebanon

you changed to shorts
and never wore the comfortable djellaba there again

you were always king year after year
the black king Baltazar
in the Christmas play

from the age of six
you were the only dark complexioned student
at the school available to play the part

when you went home to where your father
was ambassador in Iraq
you asked him shyly was it true
about you know
Father Christmas Santa Claus

he answered you quite thoughtfully
that parents wished their children to be happy
and made way

the next day you were jumping on the beds
in naughtiness with all the other kids
and one said look Arif
beneath your pillow is a card

and lo you found something you could not read
and took to show your father
who then read to you and confessed
I too can be Father Christmas
you see

and that was how
although with work of nations to endure
he took a child's question seriously
to answer both with word and act of ingenuity

following through where you had quite forgotten
the whole inquiry
or that you had ever asked

'IT IS A DREAM'

Jamal Mohammed Ahmed
rose very early every day
and sitting up with several cups of tea
began a time of reading several books

and when he rose
he felt the need to write

and his many books on government and other subjects
with collections of old Nubian tales
and also two novels that he wrote
still only in Arabic

and if you came into the room
and found him writing at his desk
he'd stop immediately and begin to tell
what he was writing of
and all his thoughts

then one day you came and he showed you
how he was preparing a new map of Africa
without sharp marks of the irrelevant borders
drawn by the colonialists

but careful undulating lines that took account
of the geography and gathering of tribal people
not dividing them with arbitrary slices
of ruler on paper

bringing war as in Kashmir and India
and many lands

man is the measure
not abstract geometry

he showed a map of Africa
that he believed could nurture peace
and he was in an exhilarated mood

but you were not entirely inspired
and feeling somewhat cynical about the possibility
said only 'It is a dream'

'that is the name' he cried out
'of the book'

SEVERITY OF UNCLE MAHJOUB

Sayyid was Fatmareya's youngest son
and even when Sayyd was grown
when she sat next to him
she held him round or rubbed his arm
or leg with an affectionate vigour

she never touched your father
except to grab a fistful
of his long silky white-with-pepper hair
when urging him to do something he had neglected
and she'd pull the fistful side to side
wobbling his head from right to left

when will you realize
he would laugh
I'm not a boy
I'm sixty years old

but Sayyid was her baby still
and she would pat and rub and hold his hand

and when his father died
he was a little child
he fastened himself to his older brothers
perhaps too much
you saw yourself how Sayyd was co-opted

he never had a voice that was his own
and he could never argue

or express opinion or a variant view
the way you were always free to jest criticize fight
with words for an idea

in fact it was the general old-fashioned way
of men to raise their songs
in solemn expectation of obedience
with totally inactive tongue

and when you went to Uncle Mahjoub's house
you had to be the one among the boys
to ask for money for the movies
it was his own movie house
and so you sat up in the loge in a special box

although you much preferred
to sit among the people

he had his own movie house
his own bank and his insurance company
that people all called Nubia
although the name was Trust Insurance Co.
or something of that sort

and of the boys
you had to be the one to say but Uncle
we don't just want to go to the movies
we want to go out after that
to have dinner at the restaurant

and he would look at you
with heavy furrowing frown a little sideways

and inquire if this request was your idea
or had the others pressed you to speak of it

and you again became aware
how all his sons
were stunned with fear of him

and you thought your Uncle Mahjoub
was a mean man

YOUR FATHER'S PERFUME

Jamal came home from Balliol
and joined the Graduate Conference
which was on looking back
the embryo of the eventual government
of free Sudan

Ismail was first president of the Conference
and then of the country

he was the one who jumped the black bull
that Fatmareya had sent for him
when he was passing through Nubia
on his way from Khartoum to Cairo

Abdullah Khalil was second president of the country
so when he sent the former president Ismail to jail
he also went to visit him a few times

Ismail was his friend

Jamal was the youngest member
and Secretary of the Conference
but more than that he gathered the gifted thinkers
he inspired gave order lofty view
and deep insight

in the new government
his work was first as university advisor

and soon ambassador to many nations
and later Minister of Foreign Affairs

and everywhere he went
he left his perfume you said
the memorable air
of his enchanted and inspiring presence

as Rumi spoke of an enlightened person
saying of being near him
'first you will notice a fragrance'
that air of shared intelligent light
uplifting all who spoke with
and then of him

he was a man so loved

he could be fierce as well
and in the years of struggle with the British
he fought with pen and ink
writing ferocious words
read by the whole of Africa

and when there was needed
in the world a leader
and first countries voted
and then regions chose
and then the continent

it was Jamal that all of Africa
desired to be Secretary General

of the whole United Nations
it was he

that year U Thant became the leader
after Dag Hammarskjöld

but Africa had spoken
and may we remember one
Jamal
among all

I KNOW HAPPINESS

your uncle Sayyid
was Fatmareya's youngest boy
and when she sat near him
she always rubbed his thigh
or roughed his arm

although she did not touch your father
except now and then
to grab his thick and silky hair
to shake his head in mock reproof
and partial threat

and he had such a temperament
if you would point out someone's malevolent remark
he would say 'oh no he didn't mean anything'
and never notice malice

in the evening when you followed him
from room to room looking after this or that
and then when he was beginning to lie down
and you were both still talking
of some curious matter
as you lifted the blankets to cover him
just as his head would touch the pillow
even as he was speaking
sudden snores announced his instant
transport unto Lethe

one may treasure the vision of such tenderness
between father and son
your love for him
equaled by his love for you

since you were young
each time you went away to school he cried
not shaking with the shoulders
but with tears along the cheek

and each time you came home from school
tears again
of strong emotions

Arif Said 'I know happiness'
he shared his composed name with you

Arif Jamal 'I know the beautiful'
it is true

RETURN TO SERRA MATTU

often if a village child went on with school
and later graduate work in foreign lands
and then came back to work for the government
and live in the teeming capital

it meant he was too overwhelmed
with soaring plans ever to go home
to his humble town
and visit former neighbors and old friends

although your father Jamal
returned quite regularly to Serra Mattu
to see how the people were getting on
and what they needed
what they felt the government was doing right or wrong

oh come and sit in this special seat we prepared for you
they said excitedly
but no he only wished to sit with them
on plain palm mats spread on the sand
and listen to their words and talk
as in old days

and when you went with him
to Serra Mattu
to stay with your grandmother and cousins
how thrilling it was in the earliest morning
to race barefoot down the sandy slopes and dunes
with all the bellowing goats

and dogs and sheep and other animals
for their first morning drink
and to swim in the fresh waters of the flowing river

while the thousand upon thousand
of high unhindered Nubian stars began to fall away
before the silvery streak of dawn
appeared along the hills

until light grew from nearly nothing
to an immensity

III.

INTELLECTUAL TENDERNESS

MERÖE

and Jamal knew all the many translations
of the Koran
from Arabic to Nubian
and how each was different from the other

there were quite a number of them
even though Nubian was not a language
ever written down
except by one state of Nubia
which was Meröe
whose language was found on the Rosetta Stone
along with Greek and the Egyptian hieroglyphs

although no one has been able so far
to decipher what the Meroitic writing said
or how each letter sounded

and Meröe was a mighty people
with magnificent square temples
that had many carvings
and many papyrus scrolls

and just before the building of the Aswan wall
the archeologists rushed forth to that ancient site
before it went beneath the water

and many said the origin
of European culture as we know it

was not so much from Greece or even Egypt
but from Meröe

they were well known for smelting iron
which expertise may have led to their demise
they undermined themselves by over-farming
and by burning their living trees in foundries

they told of God
'who was not seen by any eye
who is a companion for men and women
and whose name is Perfect Awakener'

KUSH

and your father told you how Kush
was also Nubia

and in the seventh century BC
the Kushite leader General Piankhi
rising to a threat of war from the north
surged forth with his expert archers
his finest horses and charioteers
and built a tower next to city walls
for his bow-men to shoot down from

conquering all of Egypt
over which Nubia ruled for sixty years
through the Twenty-fifth or Kushite Dynasty
during which they rebuilt many fallen temples
repaired the old papyri
and protected art

Moses was married to a Kushite woman
and he revered his father-in-law Ythro
who taught the Hebrews
how to organize themselves
as tribal people

how to travel
through the wilderness at large

INTELLECTUAL TENDERNESS

your father's scent was unforgettable
a freshness all around him
like the grass
and when he shaved
'old spice'

and was there something in his wavy hair

his arms so smooth
of yellow colour
his handsome eyes
of warm light brown

when he came home from work
you followed him around
he changed his clothes
you carefully hung up his suit
and folded his clothes
and set out the djellaba he would wear

and he told a lot of stories
you would hear news of that day
and he loved having you around
more than the older sons

he needed intellectual tenderness
you were the one

and if trouble came
he called for you

you were fourteen
and in an early hour of the morning
someone shook your shoulder roughly
waking you from sleep

it was your eldest brother Asim
he was born severe
and went into the military
growing stricter even

now he was engaged to marry
but the father of the fiancée
extremely rich
was at the final minute
after a whole year of elaborate planning
much opposed
forbidding any wedding

and the fathers met in conflict
yours protesting such a violent change of mind
when all was ready

your brother woke you roughly
saying that your father wanted you
and to everything he says
the brother warned
you must answer 'yes'
say nothing else

whenever there was trouble
your father called for you

the eldest brother was not close
your second brother Adil
was absorbed with strenuous work
in medical school

and it was something in particular
for which your father wanted only you
he needed intellectual tenderness

you were fourteen
you went into the room
your father sat up in the bed
he looked tired and sad
and beckoned you to sit near him

he could not rest
and told you the details of the stress
and what he tried to do or could do next

your brother told you
'only answer yes'

you thought of all the things your father said
and you began to speak at length
your father listened most attentively
while leaning on his elbow

you smoothed the pillow for him
helped him to lie down
and you said

you can't control
everything

he released a long long breath
and laying his head upon the pillow
finally slept

LIFE AT OXFORD

among your father's stories
was the one he told when you were older
of the way he stayed up all night
pacing wondering thinking back
to when his mother with intense instruction said

'never bow your head before anyone
except Allah
or when you go to sleep'

and 'honour is a core you must uphold'

and there he was at Oxford years later
always having loved his work of study
full of honour
always being best

he paced the room
the moon already left the leaded window
and the lamp was lit near dawn

he glanced again toward the defaming letter
on the desk
and lifted it and read

'you have dishonoured
this great university'

what had he done

the meeting was that morning
in the office of the don

they met
he stood
head lifted
then they sat

and he learned how he had been seen
at night coming back too late

climbing over the front gate
and not alone

but with a woman friend
and she was white

that was the part they found so unacceptable
for which they said
'you realize Mr Ahmed
you have soiled the reputation of a young lady
of respected English family'

he had dishonoured Oxford
and he was suspended for a month

then they had some surprise to deal with
and dishonour to digest
when shortly after their pronouncements
they received a letter
from the honoured Aldous Huxley

saying he would be the host
and Jamal would be his guest
during the entire suspension

and moreover
the white girl Catherine
was the daughter of his friend John Murry
and she would stay with them as well

and beyond that
he wanted them to know that in his domicile
there would not be a curfew

REGRET

one day driving with him
through the streets of Paris
you regret the words you said
about the letters that he often wrote
to you about his plans and study
five or six pages at a time

that they were like 'publications'
while you wanted letters from a father
much more personal

the letters metamorphosed totally
into something else
and then during troubles
the entire stack of work
was utterly lost
and you regret the words you spoke

now you regret
the words

THE RESPONSIBILITY

'you have no right'
you said

'I need the bed'
he interrupted

'you have no right to say
who is going to live
and who is not

there is only One who has the right
to make that claim
and no one knows for whom
or when the time
it could be me
even now before him'

your cousin lay
so tall and very dark
dark brown or black his colour
and too thin
with a rare illness
one in a million

you told his relatives
to gather round the hospital bed
the doctor had depressed him with bad words

you told them not to let the doctor near him
until you returned

your father had no money
so you went to find your uncle
then with funds enough
you sent your cousin off to Cairo
to stay with a sister

although the doctors gave up hope
and the relatives
all villagers
persevered to pray

he did not eat
they went on bringing food

one day his sister was preparing oil in a pan
with garlic and fresh vegetables
and some tomato

and the scent of it rose on the air
and wafted toward his fragile nostrils
and she brought food near

dark hollow eyes
glanced slowly at the plate
dark bone-thin arm reached forth
he took a morsel with thin hand
and brought it to his mouth

the change became the way he chewed
he swallowed
and he ate

since then
when the village family gathers
and they all shake hands as is their custom
in a light and fluttery way
barely touching

the moment comes when each arrives to you
and then they grasp your hand as in a vice
and grip and cling
and stare intensely in your eyes
with need or reverence

and maybe mention someone who is ill
and you say you hope they will be well
and they breathe deeply
with new breath

in a way you're horrified
and tell that you did nothing
for that cousin whom you loved
except feel a responsibility

what sacred key is this
of being

IV.

NOR BE WITH YOU

NOR BE WITH YOU

no you may not come inside the house
to fetch away your bride
from her one girlhood home
yet

first you must dip your hands
into this lovely bowl
of pure white milk

as she is pure
with whom you will share life
and pure as her fine family
treat her well
and gently

dip your hands now
into this bowl of milk

my hands are dirty

dip

my hands are
not so clean

dip

good
now that you have dipped your hands

into the milk
take a drink

he sips some milk
then each of the few gathered women
takes a sip
and there are seven turns
around the group

then he comes in
to find the modest girl
his bride
and she goes with him

'Nor be with you' is said

A WEDDING PARTY

each carrying their nabut
the whole village went forth
on donkeys mules camels
as one goes to war

Jamal and Mahjoub where there too
both on donkeys

while the older people of the group
rode smoother-gaited camels
that were easier to negotiate
for more fragile constitutions

   • • •

when Daoud Khalil
a cousin of Fatmareya
as a small child was taken to the palace
he was seen by Lady Wingate
wife of the mighty governor
an HMS emissary of Britain to Sudan
who was so pleased with his appearance
she asked him would he like to come and live
there with them
and carry her umbrella and pocketbook
for her when they went out
and he agreed and stayed with them

years later
after the independence
Sir Wingate went home to England
and Ismail arrived from the Graduate Conference
to be president of new Sudan
asking Daoud Khalil again if he would stay on
at the palace to be butler now
and he said yes

Daoud Khalil had a huge house in Khartoum
and Fatmareya liked the family there
and already had her eye on two daughters
although they went to other suitors

later she espied Zahara
meaning 'flower'
just emerging from girlhood
and Fatmareya informed the family that Zahara
was the right one for her youngest son Sayyid

and after that
when the family of Zahara was in their village Debera
where her uncle was mayor
not too far from Fatmareya's village
Fatmareya often visited
and she gave presents to the girl Zahara
spoke of her as daughter
and held her dear

then one quiet evening
a secret messenger arrived

in Fatmareya's courtyard asking her
'do you know what's going on tonight?'

do you know what is happening in Debera's village
asked the secret messenger that night

Fatmareya was all fiber of wonder
wire mouth and circle eyes

'they are having a wedding
and Zahara is the bride'

'what they are having a wedding
and did not invite me
who will bake their bread'

she is on her feet
her feet are flying to her village
she is calling out and rousing everyone
and to the fervent company she inveighs vehemently
wielding her arms

her voice reminding all how Zahara
was promised to Said her youngest boy
and will the villagers permit
this dreadful infamy of broken word

no they will not
and readily the whole company is on the road
riding donkeys mules and camels

each man carrying the nabut
the stout acacia striking staff
stripped smooth to the white wood
and cured in burning sand

and there were Mahjoub and Jamal
riding out in front

the older ones rode camels
with easier gait and with saddles
and others walked or ran alongside
each carrying the nabut
and talking in charged manner
with the ones that rode ready
to engage in war
to defend Fatmareya's rights

Fatmareya led them along roads
through starlit sand
and soon enough the tramp of hooves
was overcome by the rumble of wedding drums

a contract would be signed
at break of dawn

the wedding party came forth from the house
to confer with the armed
and uninvited guests
and finally tried to offer them
another lovely younger daughter
who would be quite grown and ready
in a year or two

and Fatmareya curled her mouth
and shook her head
while fluttering her right hand disparagingly

she didn't wish even to think about some other girl
they could try the same trick over again
so who could plan

she wanted her appropriate daughter Zahara
who was promised to Said
and she would not leave without her

and the strife went on
until the family of the girl said look
why are we arguing with them
Mahjoub is a substantial man
and Jamal is significant and so distinguished
let them have our daughter and we will not lose

don't kill any sheep cried Fatmareya
don't bake any bread
just come right away
I have everything

and the whole wedding party took to the road
on donkeys mules camels
and Zahara was married that night
in Fatmareya's house
to her husband Sayyid

and they were happy together

MEETING THE PRESIDENT

the people came to Fatmareya
meaning Fatima daughter of Reya
saying come you must come
the president will be here soon
and you must see him

what president?
the president of Nubia?

no he is president of the Sudan

I am Nubian
and I don't know him

you must see him
he is the most important man

I don't need to see him
he doesn't know me
does he come to ask my opinion?

I am Nubian
but Nubia is part of the Sudan

I will not go
but take my bull
my best bull
the black one
to where he is

and in his honour make a feast
one eighth of the bull
will be for him to eat with his dignitaries
and serve the rest to the poor

so a young man took the bull
the best of them all
the black one
and drove him twenty miles to the train
and when the president arrived
told him the bull was in his honour
sent by Fatmareya
mother of Jamal

one eighth for him
the rest was for the poor

and at the right time
he must jump over the head or tail
as was their custom

and a photograph was taken
of the president of the Sudan
in air over the bull
in honour of the gift

the poor ate well that day
and it was why so many loved
your father's mother Fatmareya

it was she who cared for everyone

V.

THE RASH ASH LAND

WESTERN DESERT

you didn't like the way the driver
hunted porcupines with tires

although the women loved to use quills
as ornament for their hair
or woven into their baskets

one night by accident
coming on a camp
the motor roused a great bull
from its slumber to a frenzy

while a woman not too tall and fairly slender
gripped the enormous creature
by the horns to try to calm him
although he had never heard such noise so near
and thrashed and slung his great head
upwards and down
and she was flung about

oh she'll be hurt you feared
but no said the driver
although afraid
the bull would never hurt her

she was to him very loved
as he to her
though the driver said it was yet needed

to turn off the motor
and he did

and then the bull grew still

a great brown bull with long extending horns
not the new kind that gives much milk
but the old lean kind
a zebu
that could outlast a drought
and thrive through hard circumstance

he thrashed his tail
and rolled his eye

THE RASH ASH LAND

your uncle Sayyid had work
to travel through west Sudan
and dig wide shallow lakes
with a machine
and line them with such stuff
that they would hold the rain

and once you traveled with him
on foray to see that realm
the driver you and he
and you sat between

the land was vast and mostly sand
and sometimes the car had to be lifted
with great effort
from its trapping sand

and once while riding across a plain
in the midst of the sand
a little bit of green appeared

and then out of the vast bare land
a woman came
and she was waving in distress

where did she come from
how was she to appear suddenly
from out of no place

and later there was standing near the way
a boy
who spoke to you with such maturity
and wore a very clean djellaba
and said that you had done an awful thing
ruining with your tires several melons
that belonged to that lady

and you said after it was settled
what melons really were there
three or four small balls of green

and Sayyid explained
how the land was dry now but soon
the rains would fall
and then the melons would grow rapidly
and he held up his arms a yard apart

they would be entirely filled with móisture
and she could squeeze out the loose interior
of fibrous matter that the goats enjoyed to eat
and it was sweet

from each mature melon
came much to drink
which could be saved until a dry spell

and how would you like
having your supply out of the tap
cut off for four days
or even three

BAOBAB

and then there was the baobab
the baobab enjoys to live alone
unlike the redwood or pine or date palm
that flings up new young beside the grown

the baobab is the thickest tree in the world
next to the sequoia
yet not too tall
with winding branches at the top

every bit of baobab is valuable
for food or medicine or wood

it is hollowed out from the top down
to hold within its girth large stores of water

and a little trap door
is cut through the bark at the bottom
from which water can be taken

in Sudan each baobab is owned and cared for
by someone or by a family
although a person passing by
may open the door to have a drink

white clustered flowers grow from the baobab
so massive and weighty
that if they grew on a date palm
that tree would crack in half

and the luffa-looking fruit
is filled with pearly sweet juice-covered seeds
so good to eat

    • • •

and then one day
although the baobab enjoys to live alone
you came upon a forest of that kind
and slept there overnight

at dawn the woods were filled
with a tremendous mind-boggling din
in every varied mode of joy or threnody
and myriad colour shape and form
of varied kinds of bird

of green and blue
yellow and white
black violet
long tail or short
straight beak or curved
bright dim great and small

and also through the baobab wood
swung many an equally loud monkey
and gazelles too were in the neighborhood

then traveling on through softening sand
the Land Rover went down a little further
than it had been wont to sink before
taking with it you and Sayyid

a thin lanky pair with not a lot of musculature
and the driver who was bigger
than the two of you together
but needed all his strength
to keep his many pounds upright
without more work to do

it became clear you needed help
and Sayyid told you how you must walk
beyond the acacia trees
and go west for five miles to find a village
which in not too long you did

several people sat outside
drinking tea with lots of sugar
that they urged you to share with them

and then they all decided that they'd help
to pull the vehicle out of the sand
but looking around
you struggled how to tell them
they were mostly old
and of the few who weren't
they were much too young

and finally understanding
they proposed you go to that more formal building
different from the huts since it had corners
and you found another group of people
sitting outside on the ground drinking tea

they too all invited you to share
though they had nothing
they would give you everything
and sugar was especially expensive
but they wished for you to have a lot

and all these men held out their hands
so many that you didn't know which way to clasp
and when one took your hand
they held on tight even with both of theirs
and then they had to ask
how was your family and how were you
oh fine
and how was your father
fine
your mother
fine

and each asked all about each one
although they didn't know them
and then you had to sit and drink
some cups of an extremely sweetened tea
until at last both groups were ready
and you all went off together
although you noticed
there was something odd between the two
and they did not communicate with each other

soon the vehicle was freed from the sand
and everyone piled in the back
roomy and open
and you asked an older man

to take your place in front
but no he wouldn't hear of it

and then Sayyid it seemed knew some of them
and asked did you pay for the goat yet
or how long now will you stay
and it grew clear that the formal building which had corners
was the prison and the people sitting out
before it were the prisoners
being confined for mostly misdemeanors
or small incidents

     . . .

then he asked others of the planting
or the sanding
the women did that work
and they had many kinds of seed
for different kinds of years
sorghum and millet and many others
ready to withstand drought or an infestation
or ready to surge forth during a long rain

or else the woman said I'm sanding
and she meant she is not planting
the whole set of seeds but only half
to see what the conditions are
and if they're good then she'll plant all
but first she's sanding

or she'll look up at the sky and say
see how the clouds are pregnant with rain
and then she'll plant the whole

the growing season was quite short
but when it came it did so
intensely and so thoroughly abundantly
that west Sudan was known
as the breadbasket of the world

that is until the long destroying drought
from the mid-nineteen seventies
through the mid-eighties
when all who could left

a parent might say I cannot pay to ride your truck
but take the child anyway
and there were maybe a million of them
with the oldest about fourteen years old
arriving in Khartoum

and people found they had to put bars
on the windows and the doors
even after some came to set up camps and schools

it is a terrible thing
you said
to have to live without love

you told so well how it might have been
if from the start the government had cared
for all those farmers to the west

and sent them the grain they needed
no matter what the cost
it never would have been as high
as what they had to pay

for those exiles in misery
longing for their desert home
and lonely for their country
where sweet desert rain fell softly
'rash-ash'
every dawn for about half an hour

VI.
THE DINKA

NILOTIC TRIBAL PEOPLE

the different tribal people
who came to market from everywhere
were of every colour
every sort of physiognomy

and there had been time enough
to sustain a great physical consistency
among the members of each group
so that if you saw them once
you'd recognize right away
a member of that clan farther off
in another section of the suk

and they were every shade
from the paler Arabian immigration
generations ago
to the deep ebony of old Sudan
having been more vulnerable to tragic capture
may their souls regain the reign of heaven

and in each tribe
distinct particularities or shapes of eye
or cheek were repeated precisely
in a diversity of scarifications
tattoos and colorations
loyally prolonged
through centuries of tribal generation

and there was one tribe
with an especially forward-drooping nose
and even their camels
had such a nose
though usual to camels
his more so than most

THE WAR OF WAY

not long before your birth
the war between the south and north
began with a massacre of many families
executed totally and in a single night
blood firing appetite for blood

the south wanted the north
out of their territory
especially the ones who taught

and forced the thought that their deity was higher
than those who were worshipped virtuously
with rapture and great reverence
for long lines of centuries
by the approximately four hundred old Nilotic tribes

remembering with searing bitterness
the role devised for them
along those ancient slave routes
which with war
has even now not ended

   • • •

and as in much of Africa
these Nilotic tribespeople had their cattle
which they dearly loved and never killed

a boy would have a bull
for which he learned to care with tenderness

from his young years
he washed the bull and fed him nurturingly
and spoke to him
even wrote poems about the beauty
of the bull and his fine attributes

he rubbed his bull over his fur entirely
with healing ash
that kept away the fleas

and when the boy grew up and had a girlfriend
he would tell her how her eyes
were even as beautiful
as the eyes of his dear calf

and one would never say
'I love you'
one said I love your eyes
I love the way you walk
I love your voice

and with that there was always more richness
fantasy
and nobility aloft

the many tribes were of great varied origin
each tribe a different shade
of tan or bronze or ebony

and many hunting people of that land
would prepare poison for the arrow
and then make a prayer

'kill swiftly
without pain'

and when an animal fell
they did not leap upon the prey
but sat nearby and made apology and explanation
that the creature would be now of new value
and go on to something better

ANIMISM

and now Sudan has revolution
over the interpretation
of Koran
or God

the south are animists
and find divinity in the bull

each son is given a young bull calf
each daughter a calf cow
to share their life

the child will tend and comb and fondly care
and clean and sleep beside the creature
sharing bed and even name
their name the same

and if the animal dies
the person will be given a new one
although the omen is severe

if a great old bull has lived quite long
and fathered many progeny
he is revered as having some divinity
within his spirit

and when a person dies
and has the luck or virtue to ascend above

how will he go to that high world of heaven
he will ride a bull it's told

and may not Brahma ride a goose
did not Elijah have a chariot

for this though and a little more
north will war against south

and they are at it still

THE DINKA

the Dinka all loved cattle
and kept thousands in their fields and corrals

killing one was anathema
although they may eat what no longer lived
except the owner of the animal
who would be too grieved
for such an appetite

the Dinka were immensely tall
and well proportioned
with much grace and poise

'the natural dignity of the African'
said Livingstone
and spoke of it often

tall Dinka hunters stood in shallows
like the heron on one leg
with the other bent sole resting
against the opposite inside knee

and holding a high upright spear
like a staff in readiness
looking out across the miles of open water
in the quiet
standing still for hours in attentive
and vast meditation
solemn and transported

far aloft
in strenuous tranquility

the Dinka were not fond of
and in fact despised their smaller
unreservedly omnivorous forest neighbors
although that tribe had contempt for all the Dinka
with their lack of table manners

all felt finer
than each other
for one thing
or another

although the Dinka
had a number of inspiring ways

THE ENGAGEMENT

your senior brother was a young man
twenty-three or twenty-four
a soldier in the army
stationed in the south
at Abyei
land of the Dinka
with the Dinka tribe

among the tallest and the darkest
and most filled with pride
of the many peoples of your country

there he became enamoured
and engaged and passionately devoted
to the elder daughter of the first wife
of Diem Majok

the Dinka chief's negotiations
for their marriage
were complex and lengthy
taking more than a whole year

though in the end
his family did not have sufficient funds
to purchase the enormous number of cattle
needed for the bride price
that the chief required

and so he lost his hope
and traveled home a bachelor soldier
sorrowful and alone

eventually he married a Nubian princess
who became known to everyone
for her heroic qualities

VII.

THE SEA SWAM TOO

THE NILE

the Blue Nile
going south out of Lake Tana
curves around and plunges
dark and roiling
to the north
through Ethiopian mountains
toward Sudan

the White Nile
pale and shallow
and immensely wide and lax
makes slow advance
along the flatland
after wandering
from Albert Lake
or the Victoria
and before that
from the mountains of Burundi
high in Central Africa

the two Niles meet
and move together
shoulder touching
shoulder
near Khartoum
each keeping to their nature
mild or turbulent
light toned or dark
until eventually they merge

becoming indistinguishable
and wind through
what was Aswan
Luxor
Cairo
not far from Alexandria

and then to the sea

CROCODILE

in fact if you were Nubian
you never said the Nile
or 'river' even

you said 'the sea'

we're going down
to the sea

he went to the sea

she rowed across
the sea

we swam in the sea
even though the many crocodiles were there
limber in the water
glimmering gracefully along the surface
partially submerged with wet
and silky-hided bark-like back
and lifted nostril

and then far behind the nose
beyond the length of jaws
the heavy-lidded
yellow old reptilian eye

would gaze laconically upon the sea
and underneath

where there were many fish to choose from
fish of all colour
pattern ornament and disguise

that vanished utterly when the free-flowing sea
became a static pool
behind the Aswan wall

and then instead of all the flourishing shapely fish
of ravishing colour nourishing flesh
and names yet unfinished
came schistosomiasis
through snail to man
or bilharziasis
through fluke to swelling liver
and looking like an advanced pregnancy

but all that happened later
the crocodile now graced the water
prowling among the myriad kinds of fish

although if there were one reptile
so rude and unruly as to come ashore
and grapple with its jaws a goat
it might find itself in not too long
entirely gutted and set in clay
above the door to guard the house

if he be too unruly
he will find himself set in the clay
among the broken crockery and bits of copper
ornamenting the immensely high façade
beneath the roof

THE SEA SWAM TOO

we swam in the deep sea
and then the sea swam too
how is that?

you never knew from year to year
where the sea would be

descending from great mountains
high up in the south
it flowed the many thousand miles
the longest river in the world

and as it flowed
it swelled and narrowed rhythmically
and also swung from west to east
and back in sinewy weave
while lifting soil from one side
and placing it on the other
so that one year you'd look outside

and see the water far away
and on your side of shore
another person's farm
that had been previously tilled
on opposite bank

and then that farmer came to you
and there were complex ways of old
to redivide and recombine

the fields with equity
considering what had been
before the water moved

that is until the British came with absolutes
of rule that fixed a plot without a jot
of comprehension of the natural shape
of the sea that swam about so
in its peregrinations to the north

old wisdom full of undulation
that allowed for flow
with change
was set aside
displaced

by arbitrary sharp rigidities
as static as the water of the lake
after the damn of Aswan

bringing much disease

HOW OLD WAS NOR

in old days
the sea swam liberally
you never knew where the sea would be
from year to year
or how high either

sometimes it brought fear
as in the year of forty-six
when floods rose
within a few feet of the door

you had to pray
to Nor

how old was Nor
how long was Nor
called Nor

as long as Nubia was Nubia
one thought

how long was that

the archaeologists tell it is a fact
that Nubians began to cultivate wild barley
eighteen thousand years ago

and we may sing with Langston Hughes
'I have known rivers

ancient as the world
and older than the flow
of human blood in human veins'

and then he sang the names

NURA

the crocodile is not inclined
to attack man
unless alarmed or very old
and out of sorts

one swam along
and hoping for the best got used
to their reptilian company
observed from time to time

there were one or two
around the watery neighborhood
and they were shy

we swam anyway
especially Nura
that terrifically vigorous woman
your aunt-in-law
who wore the Kandaka scarification
of a queen upon her handsome face

and while she swam
she carried on her head
the red enameled tray
full of fresh vegetables and yogurt
and kabida that delicious flat bread
not unlike the matzoh
and with honey and butter

unsurpassably good
ah

the sea swelled and swung around
you never knew beforehand
how high or where
and there were many lovely islands
that went down to invisibility

only the date palms you could see
although sometimes not even them

and each island belonged
to one or another family
who tilled the wealth of that alluvial earth
brought north from Ethiopian
volcanic highlands

lovingly
they tilled the earth
with love

and no matter what confusion or disorder
might sweep through the town
the Nubian fields on islands and banks
were tended in a perfect order
that no single stem of simple grass
was out of place

and this is not exaggeration
but one knew each blade
after something near a hundred and eighty centuries

of planting in that place
until with the inundation and the seaweed
every year the sea swelled up
and slowly all the islands sank

one day months later
when you had nearly forgotten
that islands were there
you saw a great white heron or a blue
land on the roof and then another
and another
or a stork or a sea mew

and one said the birds are coming back
the sea is going down
the island rose
men and women rowed across
to till and plant

then each day
Nura swam out to the family island
and on her lifted head
the metal tray painted red
was loaded up with dinner food
including soup

PLANTING

you never locked your door in those days
all along the Nubian Nile shore

since what if someone wished to visit
they should come right in

and if they pushed the door
and it stayed shut
they knew for sure that you were out
and then they saw the boomerang shaped wedge
that kept it closed
so that a goat or other creature
would not nose its way into the rooms

animals were everywhere
and made considerable noise
especially the roosters
near dawn

the night was cool
though if you stayed up late
you napped at noon

life was quiet along that Nile shore

the women wore the long jarjar
of thin black cloth that lofted lightly
on every touch of breeze
it was a garment older

than the time of pharaohs
and it had a length of train
that swept away the women's footprints
in the soft fine sand
protecting them from being followed
in old days when there were dangers
for their vulnerabilities

your mother and your aunt
and other women walking in a line
all wearing the light long jarjar

'I want you to remember who you are'
your aunt said to Fanna
meaning 'light'
when she gave a gift of that long garment
that she had made for your daughter

and you remember
how your aunt and mother
and the other women walked together
in a line down to the banks
where all the water had receded

and the woman at the front had a tall pole
with which she pressed a hole in the damp soil

and other women followed letting fall
the seeds of beans or other vegetables
that they planted
in the nutrient-rich Nile earth

their voices lofted gently on the air
it was a joyful work
a work of women
which they enjoyed

and then they sat beneath the old acacia trees
along the shore and shared their tea
and many thoughts of things that were
or things to be

and within a month
the plants were ready

'YOU NEVER WORK'

the sea went down quite rapidly
the first two weeks
then gradually more slowly
and more slowly still
and finally it grew very low

and every day the women
following the water's edge
planted seeds in the soil
you never needed to plow

alluvial soil newly arrived
on top of the old
brought all the way from Ethiopia
or even farther south
past the Victoria
from high Burundi mountains
where buffalo or elephants were wont
to graze on grass or leaves

as frequently as once the Nubian lion
stalked the shores of Nubia
and leopards were most prevalent
now hyenas and gazelles
remain by night and day

looking up from food or book
you'll see across the sand a whirling ring

of delicate gazelle in their circle dance
for perfect joy

'you do not work'
the other Sudanese accused the Nubians
with mock reproof
and so it was

women walked down in a line
to let seeds fall into the easily poled holes

bare feet enjoyed the coolness of the mud
as one roofed over the new home and womb
for each plant embryo
unwinding soon
root *apical meristem*
and shoot *apical meristem*
leading the way toward dark and light
and there was prayer to Nor

then everyone sat down
beneath the palms and the acacia trees
and had some tea

and set behind the lower lip
a little bit of nicotine leaf
and then a tiny chip of the natron
a white very porous stone
that gave an added curious bitter pungency
to the tobacco

such was the stone they used in Egypt
for its mighty siccative property
to embalm

and often there was singing

THE MADMAN

'We're drowning
we're all going to drown
the sea is going up to the hilltop'

Hassan was mad
hot helplessly insane

he could get on
but you could see
even the way he dressed in djellabas
not white or discrete blue
but flagrant red and yellow
with a flaming turban
red and green

he was eccentric
we would have to say

'we're drowning'
he went on and on
and that was tedious

until the men in business suits
with their portfolios
came to everybody's house
and relentlessly explained
'the Nile is going up
to the high hilltop'

and all the people ran from their homes
and begged each other to erase
the crazy dream from their minds
though they could not

and as for Hassan
people soon invited him for tea
and asked him important questions

will it be a boy or girl
now that they knew
he was a clairvoyant

WE DON'T WANT ELECTRICITY

—very large onions

—we don't want large onions

—you'll have land
   much more than you have now

—we don't want more land

—you'll have all kinds of luscious fruit
   such as apples

—we don't want apples
   we want dates

thus the debate went on between the government
that wished to dispossess the people of that ancient town
and the villagers

—it's a splendid place like Lebanon
   with many kinds of gorgeous trees

—we don't want Lebanon
   we want Serra Mattu

—you'll have ELECTRICITY

— WE DON'T WANT ELECTRICITY
WE DON'T WANT ELECTRICITY
WE DON'T WANT ELECTRICITY

we don't want it

THE SOLEMN MOANS

even at the time of liberation
january first
nineteen fifty-six

even then the pashas
the British and King Farouk of Egypt
were plotting to build a dam
upon Aswan

later Nasser took up the insidious cause
to press Sudan into a ruin

and the Nubian people
fought with demonstrations
through the streets of Khartoum

—where is your father

—in jail

—where is your mother

—in jail

—where is your aunt

—in jail

in those days everyone was locked in jail

police cars were too few
for the great number of arrests
so they sent taxis instead
to carry off the people
and take everyone to jail

while the demonstrations continued
with the men marching in silence
from one end of town
toward the women marching in silence
from the other end of town
all wearing black

the women saw across the way
the men coming into view
and they could no longer contain themselves
and hold in their voices

and began not cries or yells
but the low mourning tones
and the long moans of a great long solemnity

that was a moment remembered profoundly
long after Nubian land was gone

and Serra Mattu was a drowned city

EXODUS INTO EXILE

Nasser was strong
the Sudan government naïve and weak

they fought
and gave in

Nasser paid fifteen million dollars
to build the dam
that Sudan accepted from his hand

and then Sudan paid forty-five million
just to evacuate their people

in nineteen sixty
they began building the giant wall

some years later trains came
to carry off all the people

your father asked the president for leave
from his position as ambassador in Ethiopia
that he might go home to Serra Mattu
and be with his family
in the final days

the president refused
and said he would lose his post
if he returned

Jamal defied the threat
and told the president that he would be together
with his people at this time
no matter what

he went
and later the president relented

it was winter when the trains arrived
and for several days in your father's village
everyone was packing all their things
in long train cars
and then got on themselves

Nubians came from everywhere
they were in Europe and America
the Middle and Far East
to be together for the Exodus
and to share the end

the train cars were packed with people
all weeping where they sat

the engine starting up
the gasp of steam
and then a louder wail above the rest

one woman had forgotten something
so they let her out
she ran and ran across the sand
and after a long baffling wait

they saw her coming
through gray and heavy mist

she wore the long jarjar
and walked so slowly and with such conflicted step
it seemed that she was being dragged

she carried nothing in her hand
all faces looked toward her with an interrogation

she explained that she had gone back
to do what she had never left undone before

when she went out
she locked the door out of fear
of unwanted animals and beasts

THE RIVER IS ALIVE

'white horses white horses'
cried Khrushchev

when the Russians came
from glacial Siberia or Moscow
with charts and expertise and large machines
to work with turbaned Egyptians
wearing their djellabas in unheard-of heat

thousands of men struggled together
at the second cascading cataract
plunging immense blocks of concrete
into the water
while gouging a tunnel through the side

and after endless painful labor
earning a lot
more than a dollar a day
they were moving toward the set-on date
of detonation
that would change the vector of the river

men were seized with frenzy
to accomplish everything on time
and drivers wept if engines failed

thousands ran with loads of earth and rock
on head or in hand
to bolster fallen beams

for men endangered in the broken tunnel
and there was passion to achieve
the thing

when eleven years were gone
Nasser and Khrushchev detonated simultaneously
and the Nile exploded through the opening
of its new gate

'white horses
white horses'
cried Khrushchev
'the river is alive'

the river was always alive
and now is sick to death with new diseases
fishless and siltless
waters

DROWNED DAUGHTERS

the Muslims taught Egyptians
many centuries ago
not to throw bejeweled girls
on August twenty-second
into the Nile
to please the god Hapi
though they still
celebrate the day
and sacrifice
instead of daughters
bright dolls
gorgeously arrayed
that seem to satisfy
like poetry a need

VIII.

AND THERE WAS COFFEE BERRY

EACH BLADE OF GRASS AND
VANISHING FISH

forty-seven kinds of fish
became seventeen
and those just the harvestable breeds

the thirty species vanished
to block new water
to higher up and start construction
of new walls beyond Lake Nubia

the vanishing fish
the new disease uncured
by quinine from the Cinchona tree
that the Jesuits discovered in Peru
some centuries ago

the vanishing fish
lavish disease
and land that cannot yield a crop
from lack of silt
goes unremarked by damn construction mavericks
who want a new wall to block
the ancient motion of the Nile

and who want to drown the rest of Nubia
high beyond the curving Dongola Reach

to ruin ninety-nine old villages
whose ancient way is so composed

each single blade of grass is known
and in its place

NURI IS MISERABLE

Nuri is miserable
and calls from London often

'Nuri go home
I will pay' you say to him

'you only need two or three hundred
dollars a month'

'I will pay
go home' you say to Nuri
working in London to get dollars
in the cash economy to send home
to his family of wife and six children
all resettled landless out of Nubia

although the work as butler
in the traveling cortège
of a near octogenarian Arabian
consumed by lewdness alcohol and malice
was so nauseating to his sense of virtue
and Nubian truth
he was made ill

'go home Nuri'
you told him

'you Nubians
are born with a ladle in your hand
and a low stool'
the Arabs taunted

because to get money for their children's education
they often worked as butlers and cooks

and they were famous cooks

and Fatmareya would reply
'if you take someone in your house
it is because they are honest'

the Nubians were known for honesty

and for discretion
with 'their eyes in their sockets'
and 'their tongues inside their mouths'

'and Nubians are clean' Fatmareya went on
'we are used to water
and you never take a bath
your camels are more clean than you are'

but Nuri calling from London
was made ill from the atmosphere
of demoralization

'go home Nuri'
you told him

'I will pay and in a year
you will find a job

go home Nuri
go soon'

MAGDI

so Magdi as told before
was happy living in England
studying computers
when his family called him back
to help bring order to their large concerns

he complied with the request
and then remained at home
doing what was needed

he was a mild kindly
inward sort of person

then in nineteen eighty-seven
came the military coup d'état
with the army breaking down the door
and finding a small sample
of illegal foreign currency

so as a warning sign of their severity
without a trial or time to speak
they made immediate decree
to execute Magdi

many people came that night
to Magdi's mother's house
to plan a vast protest
with hundreds and with thousands
through the streets

but Magdi's mother remained adamant
it could not be
she would not give permission
no was all she said

the military took this moment to be fierce
and if the people filled the streets with fury
the military would respond with fire

she could not give permission
for these deaths

that blood
she could not answer for

she could not let her misery
extend itself into her neighbor's families
she would not do it

they had to listen to her word
and honour her intent

that night all went around the town
or stayed on the telephone
to connect influence to influence

and Magdi's mother went to the chief
of the military's wife
a woman whom she knew
and said to her we are both mothers
but the difference is that you know

how tomorrow night your son will return home
though mine may not

but for all that
with everyone desiring to help
and trying to save that one so quiet
whom everybody liked

they executed
Magdi
in the morning

he was dead

THE LADYBUG

each day you went to your small office
where you worked on a NARP
a natural resources protection group
you founded

for which you gathered funds
to show how rivers forests deserts plains
were not local phenomena only
but in fact international issues

and you connected Sudanese environmental groups
with the wider world

while others in near offices drank tea
and sweated and complained all day
how there was nothing to do there
in their work and in their country

and you said to them come with me
to the fields and to the farms and see
the work we have to do

they went with you
and found the problems of the poisoned soil
that had suffered spraying of all kinds
and when the chemical company man

will come to give instruction
he will teach that one spray
will be needed for each crop

but then you will find that for the second season
you need two sprays per crop
and then more and soon

for cotton you will have twelve sprays
of poison chemical for each crop
twelve in fifty days

in just a few short generations
farmers had forgotten centuries of wisdom

what are you having trouble with
that you resort to poison so extensively
you asked

don't spray for one cycle
and see what happens
they agreed

and when you returned to see their fields
they pointed out an infestation problem

in so few years
they could not recognize the black-dotted
round red enamel

a ladybug
the farmer's dedicated friend

AND THERE WAS COFFEE BERRY

and there was coffee berry
for the Madi
farther down from Murchison Falls
beyond the swamps where no one thrives

they planted twice a year
and said you sow one month
and then reap five
and everything the people had
the white man took

and then sold back to them
and made them work
to raise the coffee bushes in straight rows
and labor many hours

once they had all rested
without class distinctions
going out as hunters
though in general never injuring the elephant
which would harm them

until one day the white man came
with pretty coloured beads
to trade for ivory
for their billiard balls

a pair of tusks
would furnish maybe half a dozen

and the people began murdering
the great and gentle kingly creatures
by the thousands

selling out to strangers
and winning death sanguinely

WITH BRITAIN

Nubia looked toward
the north for ways

the fathers left the children
with the camels and goats
the women with the fields

and traveled north to Egypt
to work hard as cooks or janitors
or to wash the cars
in order to send money home

for the young to go to school
as Jamal went to Gordon School
and then to Surrey where he planted
side by side with Queen Elizabeth
potatoes in the field
for the war effort

and he said to her 'look
now we are the same
and equal'

and she agreed in her shy way
saying 'right right' with the high 'i'
and long-breathed
quick-cut syllables

and later he went on to Balliol College Oxford
taking careful note while studying how England
when it didn't want a foreign ruler over them
fought to the death

so that when he went home to the Sudan
the largest country on the continent
with its million square miles of land
and its eleven million people
and great quantities of tribes

he was entirely ready to fight off
the British rule at last

and then Sudan was first
of all the colonies of Africa
to become free

he fought with pen and ink
and signed his articles and letters
with the name Said
meaning 'happy'

in some respects synonymous with Jamal
which had the meaning 'beautiful'
and later he became Arif Said in print

Arif being a rare name nearly unknown
meaning 'I know'

the British left much Nubian land alone

because the banks for growing were too narrow
to make profit with a cash crop cotton field

and moreover the Nubians
Tai-Seti or 'People of the Bow'
were of a vibrant moral fiber
not too easy to overthrow or rule

needing water force
for their industrial productions
the British liked the confluence
of the Blue and White Nile higher in the south

and took the wider Sudan banks for planting cotton
where they brought Nigerians
from two thousand miles away
to do the labor for low pay

and what was independence when it came

a lot of joy
for a few days

a flag
blue yellow green

a hope and new esteem

but the country needed cash
and cotton was the imposed cash crop

they had not been impoverished
before cotton came

they grew their own food in their way
and shared a life quite filled with value
and with values
a life traded in for things
of much less worth

cotton was the job they became addicted to
and no matter what the color of the flag
the price of cotton was decided on
by financiers in London
on the Bourse

while poverty and war in the Sudan
got worse than it had ever been before
and all across the continent
the British found land
they liked more than the Sudan

such as Kenya where high mountains
full of pleasant temperatures and breezes
grew fine tea and excellent coffee

this is great the British thought
in essence continuing slavery

Uganda or Nigeria was nice for them
and even after they were gone
they ruled by setting prices for goods

cocoa in Ghana could be grown
with elaborate careful work

the farmers fought for higher prices
and refused to sell for low

the British said OK
we'll buy for what you want
but only one tenth
of the amount we bought before

and then they mixed the chocolate with milk
or peanuts cashews cocoa nuts
and every kind of filler
to avoid paying

some farmers remained poor
and many were ruined

YOU SAW HIM WHOLE

the key was in the way
you saw him whole

when you came home each afternoon
from doctorate study in agronomy
at University of Khartoum
and went immediately to his room

and when your eye met his

your eyes grow wide in telling this
with slight adjustments of focus
your eyes are wide
with open innerness and receptivity

when you saw him
then you knew without a word
all he felt

if he were well
or if he had a pain from illness
and where it was
or if he wished to have a drink
of whisky or of tea

or how the work had gone that day
or if he had a certain anger
that you did not spend sufficient time with him
the previous evening

although it wasn't always easy
when you had a wife and kid and graduate school
to share the time you wanted to

and sometimes your school friends
would come to see your wife and you

your rooms were filled with liveliness
and sometimes you would look up toward the door
and see him walking through the hall
and without slowing down at all
he would glance in

your look remembering
becomes forlorn

tears move in the breast
before a certain helplessness

he was the one who taught you
how to take life for your own
let no one borrow time from you

and then you didn't know
what all the others knew

but he told you later
how you helped heal him

as he you

IX.

MORNING IN SERRA MATTU

MORNING IN SERRA MATTU

did you hear the rooster first
or was it the muezzin

it was the rooster first
and still in darkness
before the echoing noises
of cows geese dogs
goats sheep ducks camels donkeys
composed a most momentous clamor
throughout all of Serra Mattu

at earth's equator night is long
and sharing equally with day
twelve hours of light followed by
twelve hours of dark

so that by the first hints of sun's arrival
all the animals are full of thirst
and readying with vehement cries
for a hearty drink

or was it just to celebrate
the news of dawn's return

then did the children wake
and setting down bare feet
from beds to earthen floors
already gently swept
to lead away a biting or stinging creature

the children hurried to their bowls of tea
with mostly milk
and dipped their toast
to ready for the day's first great adventure

of swinging open gates of the corrals
and racing down the long sandy slopes
and dunes with all the animals
together for their drink

and for your swim
in the cool morning Nile

but the camels stayed at home
they were too valuable to go off with the children
and they weren't in any hurry

men walked with them at a more dignified pace
and even then they did not drink out of the river
but from special troughs
prepared for them along the water's edge

and if there were a pregnant ewe or cow
an older boy would walk close by
keeping guard
so that if her time came
he could save her from an eagle or vulture
always ready up above to see or smell the blood
or from some wild cat or a hyena

the rippling river water was the perfect temperature
to freshen and to soothe

and all the children and animals
shared joy and much enchantment

by the time the straggling crowd came back
the sun was hot

CONFUSION AND ORDER

when you went north to Serra Mattu
from the city of Khartoum
to stay awhile with your grandmother
and cousins

then you were quite upset at the confusion
'what are you doing?'
the cousins called

'look they're getting all mixed up'
you lamented
as you tried to separate and redirect
the neighbor's ewes and rams from yours
while they were all hurrying
together in a commingling group

'don't worry don't worry'
they tried to reassure you

but you thought 'you say that now
although just wait till we return
and then you'll see what the trouble is'

the animals came back with all the children
in a straggling herd of different kinds
from different homes

and then miraculously you saw
how just before the gates

each animal knew its path and curved away
to enter at the proper place

and you amazed began to think
how animals had their own souls
and their own knowledge

and all of them returned correctly
except for one angry old dangerous sheep
who once had injured a small lamb
and even knocked a child down

Fatmareya had gone to the neighbor's house
and said 'your ram is mad
the old one with the gnarled horn
I want to buy him'

which she did
and soon invited all those neighbors
for a feast of meat
which was a food not eaten very often
and even then one got only a little bit
since each shared some
and nothing could be left
there were no refrigerators

and we can see Fatmareya's famous wisdom
in this moment of potential conflict

she did not return the anger from the ram
with hers against the owner
but simply purchased him

transforming as in alchemy
some growing grudges
into a shared revelry
quite peaceful

THE RABBIT IN THE MOON

so when the rooster crowed
soon followed by an intensity of noise
from all the other animals and children

racing together to the sea
then they were joined by swirling birds
of many kinds

whirlwinds of swifts
that rose and dove wildly among them
swerving sharply up again

white cattle
egrets with slow wings who flew with them
or rode along on cattleback

and all the birds were calling too
with thrilling cries round the shore
where many drank and many plunged right in
and swam about
all splashing and some calling out

and then all around across a vast expanse
of sand and sea
the changing of the guard occurred

the rabbit in the moon dissolved
the moon itself grew tissue thin
or wandered off

the myriad stars resolved themselves
those high unhindered Nubian stars
composed themselves by growing dim
before the milky rim of dawn
within the dark

that suddenly from
wide hill horizon rose like fire
through the immensity
of the Eastern sky
with orange above the red
that rode upon a darker layer

and hearts of all the creatures
and the children were cheered already
by the ringing splashes
of shared freshening water
drank in the blessing of the newborn light

and everywhere they turned to look
was heaven

• • •

in those days there was one silky little kid
black brown and white
that you held especially dear
and carried with you everywhere

until the grownups had to call to you
from time to time to let him go
back to his mother and have milk

as you would like to go
sometimes oppressed by choking cities
or stranger's insolence

back to mornings in Serra Mattu

ACKNOWLEDGMENTS

There are not enough words to express my gratitude and appreciation to Dave Eggers for his support of my work. His review of an earlier iteration of this book provided the impetus for the wonderful experiences to follow.

I am particularly grateful to Dominic Luxford, best ally any writer could ever have. I especially admire his wide knowledge of the language and his love for poetry. I do not think I would have been able to go through the countless hours of editing without his refreshing views and positive reinforcement.

I also thank Jesse Nathan and his wonderful sense of the word, the research and the person that he brought to the table. His continued encouragement and genuine interest in my book brought a thrill and pleasure to my heart.

I thank my wife, Eiman, for her support and encouragement. I thank her for this and more.

This book is dedicated to E.G. Dubovsky. Without her this book would not have been.

ABOUT THE AUTHOR

Arif Gamal was born in 1949 in Khartoum, Sudan. His father was among the first diplomats inducted into the Ministry of Foreign Affairs after Sudan's independence. During his childhood, Gamal followed his father throughout the Middle East, the United Kingdom, the United States, and Ethiopia. In his early teenage years, he attended Brummana High School, a Quaker school, in Brummana, Lebanon, and later returned to Khartoum for his college degree.

In 1975, Gamal left for France for his postgraduate degree, and in 1980 he received his doctorate in environmental sciences from the University of Montpellier. Gamal then returned to Sudan, where he worked and taught until the military coup d'état in 1989, during which period his cousin was tragically put to death by the military. In 1991, Gamal accepted a research position at University of California at Berkeley as a Senior Fulbright Fellow, and he has lived with his family in Northern California ever since.

Gamal has been a panelist and keynote speaker for many national and international conferences, seminars, and workshops focusing on environmental issues, from Nicaragua to the Netherland. In the early '90s he lobbied in both the House and the Senate for the African Trade Bill. He was awarded the National Resources Defense Council's Stephen Duggan Environmental Award in 1989. Since the building of the Aswan Dam and its devastation of Nubia, Gamal's interests have centered on local and global efforts to support Nubia, the Nubian culture, and all the people affected by displacement from the many dams built on the Nile. This book is one of these efforts to raise national and international awareness of the injustice to, and plight of, displaced populations around the globe.

THE McSWEENEY'S POETRY SERIES

McSWEENEY'S
POETRY SERIES

The McSweeney's Poetry Series is founded on the idea
that good poems can come in any style or form, by poets
of any age anywhere. Our goal is to publish the best,
most vital work we can find, regardless of pedigree.
We're after poems that move, provoke, inspire, delight—
poems that tear a hole in the sky. And when we find
them, we'll publish them the only way we know how: in
beautiful hardbacks, with original artwork on the cover.
These are books to own, books to cherish, books to loan
to friends only in rare circumstances.

>>>———<<<

SUBSCRIPTIONS

The McSweeney's Poetry Series subscription includes
our next four books for only $40—an average of $10
per book—delivered to your door, shipping included.
You can sign up at store.mcsweeneys.net